Unpack Your Dreams with a Life Coach You Can Afford

A 30-day guide to moving forward

CINDY MOSLEY

UNPACK YOUR DREAMS WITH A LIFE COACH YOU CAN AFFORD : A 30 Day guide to moving forward

Copyright © 2017 by Cindy Mosley

All rights reserved. Printed in the United States of America. No part of this book may be used or reproduced in any manner whatsoever without written permission except in the case of brief quotations embodied in critical articles or reviews.

Book Formatting by Derek Murphy @Creativindie

For information contact :

CiMo Inspirations

P. O. Box 258

Hallsville, TX 75650

http://www.cindymosley.com

ISBN: 978-0-692-05074-3

CONTENTS

INTRODUCTION ....
DAY 1: WAKING UP 5
DAY 2: THE MEASURE OF THINGS 11
DAY 3: TRUTH BE TOLD 14
DAY 4: SET YOUR DESTINATION 18
DAY 5: UNWANTED PASSENGERS 21
DAY 6: THE WINDOW SEAT 25
DAY 7: A DAY OF REST 28
DAY 8: ON THE ROAD AGAIN 30
DAY 9: PLUG IN THE EAR BUDS 33
DAY 10: TAKING INVENTORY 36
DAY 11: CLEAN OUT THE CLOSETS 38
DAY 12: A NEW VIEW 40
DAY 13: CAUTION: WALL AHEAD 42
DAY 14: ANOTHER DAY OF REST 44
DAY 15: SPEED BUMPS AND WALLS 46
DAY 16: STARTING AGAIN 48
DAY 17: SHARPENING SKILLS 51
DAY 18: SEND OUT INVITATIONS 53
DAY 19: PLAN A LAUNCH PARTY 56
DAY 20: NEW EQUIPMENT 58
DAY 21: REST FROM YOUR WORK 61

DAY 22: REFLECTION 62

DAY 23: THE POWER OF "NO" 65

DAY 24: GIFT OF DELAYS 67

DAY 25: SHARE THE WEALTH 69

DAY 26: STEPPING OUT 71

DAY 27: LEGACIES AND LEGENDS 73

DAY 28: PAUSE 75

DAY 29: FORWARD TOGETHER 76

DAY 30: LAUNCH DAY 78

5S SUCCESS STRATEGIES 83

ABOUT THE AUTHOR 85

INTRODUCTION

The beginning of a journey often starts with a push off. Whether we are taking a journey in a vehicle or a journey in our lives, we are usually propelled forward with a jolt. How we end the journey has nothing to do with how we started. But what does matter is what we do when we hit a bump in the road or hit a barrier. We choose the direction we travel as a reaction to something that went wrong or an intense desire to be different than we were before. This is true for any journey or dream.

People who know me know that I have lived an unusual life. It has been a good life full of pivotal moments that have taken me from one plateau to another. In between those plateaus have been some valleys that have shaped who I am as an individual, wife, parent, educator, and mentor. The plateaus are marked with moments of elevation and fulfillment of several dreams. I can recall dreaming about adopting children as a young girl. I am now the parent of two "chosen" children in my family and I have adopted numerous children with my heart who call me "mom".

I also dreamed of helping women who were being abused by their intimate partners, and became an educator for a women's crisis center where I facilitated support groups for batterers and wrote curriculum for the women's support groups. This dream job was instrumental in pushing me to fulfilling another dream—becoming a teacher. I'm not teaching the subject I dreamed of teaching, but I am teaching. I wanted to be a writing teacher.

I developed a love for writing while in junior high school. Writing was a great way for me to express myself, especially when I was feeling lonely and depressed. I was good at writing essays and poetry. When I decided to pursue a teaching career, I wanted to help young people learn how to express themselves with writing so I set my sights on teaching English Language Arts. To my disappointment, the only job I was offered was a math teacher position and I took it. What a wonderful opportunity for growth. It wasn't long before I was teaching my math students how to use writing to remember difficult math concepts and using writing as a way to assess what they knew.

Writing books is another dream fulfilled. I started writing books in high school, but never took the initiative to publish. In fact, I hit what I think is a significant roadblock on my way to becoming an author. Someone I care about laughed at my desire to write a book. It was one negative statement and inconsiderate observation that made me shove the book I had written in a drawer to never pick it up again. I didn't stop writing altogether, but I did trash the book I was working on. I began to feel self-doubt and tell myself that I didn't have anything to say that would create interest.

Recently I was organizing my library of books and found a journal I had packed away. I was amazed that I had written over thirty pages of poems and songs. I had literally packed away a dream. Some of the poetry in that book dates back to the early 1980's and I am now publishing them in books and online. I have heard people say that all you have to do to fulfill your dreams is to start. I believe that statement is true to a degree. Starting may be the easiest part of fulfilling a dream, but what I realized after starting on this writing and publishing journey is that the biggest killer of dreams is not knowing what to do when you hit a wall. Certain walls will cause some people to pack up their dreams and store them away for a later date or simply leave them packed away to gather dust.

This book is my challenge to you to unpack your dreams. This 30-day journey comes with challenges and resources that will help you maintain momentum as you unpack your dreams and experience the life you always wanted. You can hire a life coach or you can join me on my journey. Whatever path you take, traveling with a partner makes the journey more interesting and less overwhelming especially when you hit a wall. A life coach will encourage you to keep focused on the road ahead and point you to resources along the way. But there are times when you have to encourage yourself. You will need to become your own life coach. UNPACK YOUR DREAMS is a life coach you can afford. The principles and resources in this book will help you when you hit walls on your journey. Let's take this journey together over your walls, around your walls or to use those walls to help you get moving forward.

Day 1
WAKING UP

MAKING significant life changes is like gradually waking up from a long and peaceful night sleep in a hotel room at the end of a vacation. The sun slowly lightens the sky teasing your eyes awake through the subtle opening in drapes that never really close. Eventually you quit fighting and succumb to getting up to face the day that lies ahead. You knew the daylight was coming and you knew you are at a temporary destination for a temporary purpose, but you wanted to delay getting up just a little bit longer. Or maybe you wanted to stay in bed because you did not want to face what was ahead.

That is how it happened to me. I woke up one day and knew that I had delayed fulfilling my publishing dreams long enough. I am destined for more and I am going to have it all. At first, I had no idea where to start, so I did what I usually do when I want to make something happen--I started a journal.

Journaling is my go-to action for many things. I have a journal for my writing ideas. I have a prayer journal. I have a journal of projects I want to assign my math students. When I think about it, my blog is a journal of the things I want to say to the world.

You may think my journaling is a little extreme, but there is research out there that suggests journaling is good for physical, mental, and intellectual well-being. Also, journaling is one of the oldest writing strategies in the world. Without journaling, the Bible would not exist.

I can attest that journaling helps me relieve stress, organize my ideas, and provide a place for me to be creative. Journaling has helped me through difficult times in my life and continues to be a great resource for organizing my thoughts and goals. I even have art journals that include sketches and paintings that reflect my need to escape and relax.

Selecting a Journal

Journaling is one of the least expensive things you can do to get your life moving forward. Your first step to moving forward is to start a *Moving Forward Journal*. Yes, it's time to awake from your sleep and get busy fulfilling your dreams. Get up and head to your local discount store for a journal. You don't have to choose a designer model, but because you are making a move toward your future, why not start with something special. Pick something eye catching, something that will tempt you to pick it up. If you cannot afford a fancy model, I suggest choosing something as simple as a spiral notebook or a composition book. If you want to make it look special, decorate it. I like using journals with lines, but you may prefer blank pages. It doesn't matter the style. What matters is taking the first step.

The most inexpensive journals are the free ones you create yourself on your computer. If you are computer savvy or not so savvy, journaling on your computer is as simple as opening a word processing document and typing. You may even find journal templates online or within the software on your computer. If you're really feeling like making a drastic move, try starting a blog.

What to Write

- Find a thinking spot that will serve as your journaling space. Start with writing a motivational message to yourself inside the front cover or on the first page. Make it the first thing you see when you open the journal. There will be days ahead when you may not want to write, but if you are serious about moving forward it is important to establish routines and commit to them. So, write yourself a motivational message that will be there for you when you need it, when you feel like quitting.

- Make a list of your goals. What have you always wanted to do? What dreams have you packed away? It's time to make a plan to do them. When you set goals, give them a timeline. I would start with something short term, something that could be done without much preparation or stress. Then move to things that can be done with a little effort in a few months. Finally set a goal that you know it may take you a while to accomplish. Setting goals in progression makes the task of moving forward seem less overwhelming. When you've recorded your dreams, leave your journal in your thinking spot and take a walk. Walking is not only good for your health it is also good for thinking. I have come up with some really good ideas while taking a short walk.

- When you return to your journal tomorrow, start making a list of what you need to do to accomplish your goals beginning with the short-term goal. Give each goal a time line and write down what success looks like to you. You want to give yourself something to look forward to.

- Write about your feelings while accomplishing your goals and address setbacks. I suggest you find motivational messages to write each day. For me, I write scriptures and quotes from some of my favorite authors and speakers. When I feel discouraged, I return to those messages to keep up momentum.

- Record ideas that may come to mind even if you don't plan to use them right away. This always helps me when I run out of fresh ideas. I have a reference list to turn to for getting on track again.

Things to Avoid

- Negative self-talk. Nothing can kill a dream faster than negative thinking. We can talk ourselves out of things that appear to be out of our reach or we can choose to encourage ourselves. When you have setbacks or run into a wall, use journaling to process future action rather than beat yourself up for the delay in your progress. I've learned to celebrate my setbacks and use them as learning opportunities.

- Internalizing negative messages from others. You will encounter people who don't see your dream as valuable as you do. They may try to tell you that your plans won't work or that you are reaching too high. Use their comments as a checkered flag for pushing yourself forward. Don't let the enemy of your dreams talk you out of the future you desire. Write down three positive replies for every negative message you hear. Every time you want to rehearse their words, turn to the positive ones instead.

- Comparisons. We can become discouraged when gauging our success using someone else's idea of success. We will address comparisons later. But for now, when you start comparing yourself to others, start a list of your own attributes and how the success of your dreams will bless someone else. (See Chapter 2)

For more on journaling I recommend the following resources.

https://michaelhyatt.com/daily-journal.html

https://psychcentral.com/lib/the-health-benefits-of-journaling/

http://www.creative-writing-now.com/how-to-write-a-blog.html

Day 2
THE MEASURE OF THINGS

When we measure physical things, we use tools like rulers, meter sticks, and scales. But when we measure our personal success, we tend to use the strangest tools. The most popular tool I've encountered is "comparisons". We compare ourselves to popular celebrities, political leaders, and many times our neighbors. We may even compare ourselves to the image of success taught to us by significant people in our lives.

It is important to use the correct tools when we measure things. We wouldn't use a cooking thermometer to check if our sick child has a fever. We wouldn't use a ruler to measure the length of a piece of property. And we certainly wouldn't use a grocery scale to check if we have been successful on our latest attempt to lose weight. We live in a competitive society where we are expected to out-do our neighbors. In order to compete, we compare where we are to where they are. If we see any distance between us and them, we start to doubt ourselves and start trying to catch up.

I have had conversations with several people who expressed the desire to write a book or start a business. They seem to be genuine in their desire, but begin to talk themselves out of their ideas because they have seen similar books and businesses with the same or similar ideas as theirs. They think no one will want to read or engage with them. I encouraged them to examine their ideas closely and make a list of the unique aspects of their ideas. No two people are exactly alike and when we put our own unique touch on things, neither are our ideas. We all have a special purpose for living that involves influencing the world around us with our individual talents.

Instead of comparing yourself to people who have already accomplished what you are planning, try celebrating their success. Have a conversation with them and find out how they succeeded. You may learn something that can help you reach your goals. You should also avoid comparing your past to your future. If you have made mistakes you are not proud of, don't allow them to keep you from starting over. Remember every day is a fresh start and you aren't hopeless until you breathe your last breath.

TODAY'S JOURNAL ENTRY

Reflect on the following:

- Are you guilty of comparing yourself to others?
- What unique qualities do you have that you would like to share?
- What is your area of influence (education, health, business, finance, ministry, or community service)?

RESOURCES RELATED TO OVERCOMING COMPARISONS:

Over It.: Conquering comparisons to live out God's plan by Kristine Brown

How to Overcome Social Comparison by Susie Moore
http://www.huffingtonpost.com/susie-moore/comparison_b_4646013.html

How to Stop Comparing Yourself to Others—and Feel Happier! by Preson Ni, M.S.B.A.
https://www.psychologytoday.com/blog/communication-success/201409/how-stop-comparing-yourself-others-and-feel-happier

Day 3
TRUTH BE TOLD

WHEN I facilitated support groups for batterers one of the first things, we worked on was the truth. The men had to tell the truth about the incident that got them arrested without blaming or minimizing. The experience was challenging for them, but eventually we were able to use the truth to learn what was at the core of their abusive behavior and what triggered their behavior that lead to the arrest. We would then use those discoveries to identify alternate reactions to triggers and to set goals about how to move forward without blaming their past, their partners, or others for setbacks. Having the men tell the truth about themselves was essential for them to make the changes needed to keep their families safe and to stay out of jail which was a dream of sorts for many of the men who had multiple arrests for the same behavior. Their goal was to avoid going to prison.

Packing away our dreams isn't the same as abusing our family, but some of the reasons for delaying our dreams are similar to those of the men I worked with. Most men in the group learned from their fathers how to treat their partners. We either delay our dreams because at some point in our childhood, we may have been told what our dreams should be or we dream of being the opposite of someone who disappointed us.

Our parents may have decided our future for us. My parents started when I was young preparing me for an office job. I received my first typewriter when I was six years old. Their dreams of their daughters having careers was planted in my mind and I did get a job in an office when I was older. I eventually wanted more and the rest is history. I am now doing what I love to do. I learned to type, but I use my typing skills for writing books, creating lessons, and publishing my blogs.

We also pack away our dreams because of fear or insecurities. I explained earlier that I delayed writing a book because someone laughed at me. I was afraid others would laugh at me as well. I wasn't sure that what I was writing was good enough and I delayed other dreams because I was afraid of rejection.

Upon further reflection and research, I discovered the reason many people abandon their dreams or put them on hold is one of the following:

- Fear of failure
- Fear of rejection
- Unrealistic expectations
- Unmet needs
- Lack of resources
- Lack of knowledge
- Lack of direction
- Lack of support

If your truths are one of those listed above, you can start working around them by surrounding yourself with people who will support you, and start researching for resources and information about what it takes to accomplish your goals. Examine your reasons for wishing to fulfill your dreams and be certain what you are working for is beneficial and not hurtful. For every reason you have put your dreams on hold, find three reasons why you should begin pursuing them.

Today's Journal Entry

Reflect on the Following:

- Why have you delayed fulfilling your dreams?
- Is there some fear you need to face and release?
- Are you blaming someone for putting your life on hold?

Resources for Getting Past Delays

How to Conquer the Fear of Failure – 5 Proven Strategies by Vaness Loder
https://www.forbes.com/sites/vanessaloder/2014/10/30/how-to-move-beyond-the-fear-of-failure-5-proven-strategies/#54510cca1b78

Downside Up: Transform rejection into your golden opportunity by Tracey Mitchell

Destined to Be: Nine keys to discover your purpose while unlocking your potential by Jeff Barnhardt

Day 4
Set Your Destination

HAVE you ever just jumped in the car and started driving with no destination in mind? Or have your ever walked into an airport to take a trip without knowing where you were going? I've only taken a spontaneous road trip, but it was partially planned and I had a destination in mind. The problem is, I was not prepared. I hadn't packed anything for me or my three children. I had to buy clothes and toiletry items for the four of us. I admit that although it was really fun, careful planning would have saved me some money.

Knowing your destination or your dreams can not only save you money and time, it can also save you stress and heartache. There is nothing more miserable than working at a job that you hate or not being qualified for the job you want. I remember very clearly when I knew I really wanted to be a teacher. I was volunteering at a local elementary school. I had so much fun interacting with the children. I loved seeing them figure things out. When I searched for job openings at the school, I realized I was not only unqualified to teach, I was not qualified to be a teacher assistant either. I was crushed. But I soon learned that my dream was not completely out of my reach. I just needed to get the qualifications. Knowing what I wanted was the beginning of me moving forward. I enrolled in college to get one degree and didn't stop until I had the credentials, I needed to become a teacher. It took me three careers to get here, but I made it.

Taking that first step of faith and enrolling in college has led to new dreams and learning new things about myself and my potential to help others fulfill their dreams. <u>You can have what you desire as well.</u> I've been telling you the story of my journey as if I started and made a straight path to my dream, but I didn't. I got married right after high school and used marriage as an excuse to put my college education on hold. I didn't start my college education until I was thirty and didn't become a teacher until I was forty. Once I determined my destination, I kept going until I got there. You can do the same.

TODAY'S JOURNAL ENTRY

Reflect on the following:

- What is your desired destination?
- What do you need to do to get to where you want to be?
- What resources do you need to reach your destination?

RESOURCES FOR KNOWING AND REACHING YOUR DESTINATION

The Purpose Driven Life: What on Earth am I here for? By Rick Warren

Helping You Find Your Life Purpose by Susan Biali, M.D.
https://www.psychologytoday.com/blog/prescriptions-life/201311/helping-you-find-your-life-purpose

How to Fulfill Your Dream: Oprah's LifeClasss
http://www.oprah.com/oprahs-lifeclass/how-to-fulfill-your-dream-video

Day 5
UNWANTED PASSENGERS

YEARS ago, I rode the bus from Longview, Texas to San Diego. California with two friends. We bought our tickets and boarded the bus. We were paying customers, but along the way some people who had not purchased a ticket boarded the bus. Eventually the bus stopped and security escorted the unwanted passengers off the bus.

As we are working to fulfill our dreams, we will encounter unwanted passengers as well. Procrastination, distractions and doubt (PD&D) are passengers we must eject immediately upon detection. When I think about procrastination and distractions, I always think about the ant and the grasshopper fable. The grasshopper put off preparing for winter while the ant worked very hard to be ready for hard times. There is also a biblical lesson about an ant in the book of Proverbs. It says, *"ᵃThey have no leader, chief, or ruler, ⁸ but they store up their food during the summer, getting ready for winter."* The ants don't have someone standing beside them or in their faces telling them to "Get busy", "Get to work", "You've got this". They instinctively know if they want to survive, they need to start storing up for the hard times.

I will admit that when I started this book, I was on a roll until the end of Chapter 4. For some reason, I lost the urge to write. I was sleepy all the time and I wanted to paint or crochet or read. I was doing everything except getting what was in my heart on these pages. I wanted to call it procrastination, but it was the "D" twins—doubt and distractions. I doubted anyone would want to hear what I had to say and I doubted I could get this book finished before the end of the month (an unrealistic expectation). In my doubt, I allowed distractions to pull me from my focus.

I wrote a poem to encourage myself when the D's try to hitch a ride on my journey forward:

RISE UP AND BE YOU

> You are unique, created for something wonderful.
> Your place in this world was decided long ago.
> What you think is not special
> is just what was missing
> Until you were born.
> Rise up and be
> you!

When I want to eject procrastination, doubt, and distractions, I tell myself, "Rise up and be you", pray for guidance, turn on some uplifting music, and start where I left off. These four things serve as my "eject" button for PD&D.

Kick those unwanted passengers off your "dream bus". Rise up and be you—do your thing!

Today's Journal Entry

Reflect on the Following:

- What are the unwanted passengers trying to hijack your dreams?
- When you want to get back on track, what can you do to eject those unwanted passengers?
- What is your motivation song, prayer, or message?

Resources for Overcoming PD&D

Elizabeth Lombardo Ph.D.
Better Than Perfect: 11 Ways to Overcome Procrastination
Easy tips to stop putting things off.
Posted Mar 07, 2017
https://www.psychologytoday.com/blog/better-perfect/201703/11-ways-overcome-procrastination

Procrastination

https://www.hopefortheheart.org/pdfs/OLQR-pr-Procrastination.pdf

Day 6
THE WINDOW SEAT

HAVE you ever traveled with someone that made the journey to somewhere wonderful totally miserable? You were so miserable that when you got to your destination, all you could think about was dreading the journey home. You may have even been tempted to return home in a different car. Or maybe you decided to stay put so that you wouldn't have to face the experience again. Instead of wallowing in the miserable emotions that come from the struggle, try changing your view of the journey.

I have a friend who gets car sick if she rides in the backseat. If she rides in the front, she can see out the window ahead of her. She said it helps to see where she is going. The journey to our dream destination comes with passengers I call peace killers—fear, dread, and anxiety.

These peace killers can block our view of the road ahead. Fear can trick us into thinking we have chosen the wrong path. Dread is another form of fear and deceives us into believing we are destined to fail. Anxiety is fear masked as worry that it is too late to fulfill our dreams. All three of these emotions can shipwreck our plans and cloudy our vision. This is where creating a vision board can help.

The term vision board reminds me of one of my favorite Christmas movies starring Queen Latifa. In *Last Holiday* Queen Latifa plays a shy and passive sales person who is secretly in love with another sales personnel. She keeps a "Book of Possibilities" that catalogs her hopes and dreams. When she is diagnosed with a terminal illness, she pulls her book of possibilities from its hiding place and begins fulfilling her dreams. She shook off her fears and lived each day to accomplish her dreams.

A vision board doesn't have to be a "board", it can also be created as a book or even a digital poster. It is something you can display to help you keep your eyes on the prize. I create the covers for my book ideas to give me a visual of possibilities. I have sketches and drawings of places I hope to visit or to have as inspiration for poetry. The purpose of the vision board is to have a focal point when fear, dread, and anxiety come to take your attention away from your destination. John Maxwell says we need to starve our fears and feed our dreams. What better way to feed our dreams than to have something displayed to give us courage to keep moving forward?

Today's Journal Entry

Reflect on the Following:

- What type of vision board would you create?

- What would you include on your vision board?

- What other strategies could you use to overcome fear, dread, and anxiety?

Resources for Overcoming Fear, Dread & Anxiety

How to Create an Empowering Vision Board by Jack Canfield

http://jackcanfield.com/blog/how-to-create-an-empowering-vision-book/

Overcoming Anxiety Through Spiritual Warfare by Carol Peters-Tanksley MD DMIN

https://www.amazon.com/Overcoming-Anxiety-Through-Spiritual-Warfare/dp/1629990973

Day 7
A Day of Rest

FIRST of all, read Day 8 before reading this.

Now let's define rest.

> *Oxforddictionary.com says, "Cease work or movement in order to relax, sleep, or recover strength; allow to be inactive in order to regain strength or health."*

Resting from this journey of unpacking our dreams means giving ourselves time to reflect on what we've accomplished so far. There are days when I have to force myself to take a break. I have to schedule time off from "doing" in favor of "receiving". Being intentional about resting is not only good for creativity, but it is also physically beneficial. One word of caution, not scheduling time off can cause burnout and not starting again on schedule can delay our progress.

Taking a rest from your labors is needed in order to be most productive. Writing is my passion and I get such a rush from creating poetry and stories. I would put pen to paper every day, but I discovered when I take a break to rest or paint, I get inspired. I even find inspiration in visiting a friend's house, taking a walk, or just relaxing with a good book. My most productive inspiration time is when I pray and meditate on the dream that is living in me.

Today's challenge is to stop "doing" your dream and allow yourself time to reflect on what you have accomplished so far. Share your dream with someone who will encourage you. Take time to encourage someone else to unpack their dreams.

Today's Journal Entry

Reflect on the Following:

- What did you do to relax?
- How did you share yourself with others?
- Write a plan for next week's day of rest.

Day 8
ON THE ROAD AGAIN

I PARTICIPATE in an online inspiration group and during one of our conference calls, there was a young lady who poured out her heart that she has lost her way. She was back in the group because she needed the support. Our group coach was very understanding and acknowledged that all of us have times when we stop but fail to remember to start again. She declared that we all should press our "refresh" button and join our returning member in starting over, starting fresh.

When I started this project, I was so motivated and determined to have this done within six months. Well, that didn't happen. In fact, I started getting stuck at the end of chapter three. I took a rest, but I got caught up in my emotions and I let stress at work steal my focus.

That one little break caused me a very long setback. Then I started wondering if I was doing the right thing in starting this project. Would this one be successful? What if I unpacked the wrong dream? What if this really is "a dream"?

During my rest, I forgot to reflect on how much I had accomplished. I forgot to plug into my support system. I forgot to start where I stopped as soon as possible. That is when the voices started creating roadblocks. When I finally did make connection with an encouraging friend, my passion for this project was re-ignited. I hit the "reset" button and began my journey again.

I went back to the message I had written to inspire myself. I found my motivational scripture. I went back to the place where I wrote down my dreams to get my perspective back. I went back to the source of my dream and that is how I got back on the road to my destiny.

Your challenge today is to get going again. If you rested and started immediately, great. But if you walked away and took a detour, welcome back. It's not too late to begin again.

Today's Journal Entry

Reflect on the Following:

- What do you do when you have a setback?
- How do you begin again?
- Make a plan for what you will do if you get stuck or need to build momentum after a break.

Resources for Getting Back on Track

Developing Resilience
https://www.skillsyouneed.com/ps/resilience.html

8 Ways to Create Momentum in Your Life
http://www.success.com/article/8-ways-to-create-momentum-in-your-life

Momentum for Life by Mike Slaughter
https://www.cokesbury.com/digitalstore/download/momentumforlifech1_os.pdf

Day 9
PLUG IN THE EAR BUDS

ON the journey to our dreams we are going to run into sound barriers. I am not referring to the sonic boom we used to hear when a jet broke the sound barrier. I am referring to the noise and voices of people who don't understand our dreams.

Not everyone is going in the same direction as us. They don't see what we see. They cannot hear what we hear. Because they are on the outside looking in, they may try to discourage us. They may have good intentions in trying to keep us from failing. Then again, they may be determined to keep us from transforming into someone they don't recognize. It doesn't matter what their motives are, if we allow negative reports and advice to cause us to stumble, we might not reach our destinations.

I allowed someone's negativity to slow me down for over 30 years. When I started again, I simply plugged in my ear buds and refused to stop. I have been told to slow down, but I cannot finish if I don't keep moving. I tune in to my favorite radio stations now and move to the beat of my music. Music drowns out the noise and voices declaring "You can't" and "You shouldn't".

One of the best ways to get past negative messages is to surround yourself with people who are doing what you are doing or have already succeeded at it. Having a support system with similar interests and goals will help you keep your dream alive. You might even find resources and guidance to help when you need direction.

I recently wrote this poem to encourage my friends to keep moving forward when they get blind sided by discouraging messages.

Rise Above the Noise

Rise above the voices.
Rise above the noise.
Set your mind to understand
What the Father enjoys.

He waits for your fellowship.
He's calling you to Him.
He's calling you away
From what makes your vision dim.

Rise above what used to be
From what kills your fruit and land.
Allow your Creator to shape your future
Into the future He has planned.

Don't let the enemy of your dreams hinder your progress. If you started the journey, you will complete it if you are patient and have faith.

Today's Journal Entry

Reflect on the Following:

- What can you do when the enemy of your dreams try to hinder your progress?
- Make a plan for how you will respond when you hear discouraging words about your dream.

Resources for Encouraging Yourself

8 Ways to Deal with Family and Friends Who Don't Support Your Dreams by Erica Nicole
http://www.huffingtonpost.com/entry/8-ways-to-deal-with-family-and-friends-who-dont-support_us_5911eb90e4b0e070cad70910

Ways to Encourage Yourself
http://rachelwojo.com/ways-encourage-yourself/

Encourage Yourself
http://www.goodfinding.com/encourage-yourself.html

Day 10
TAKING INVENTORY

EVERY successful retail company keeps a list of inventories. If they didn't, how would they know what they had to sell or what had been sold? Today, let's look at what we have to offer.

I knew I could write poetry and I enjoyed writing essays when I was in school. I know that's just unbelievable to some people, but I do love to write. I enjoy the process of researching an idea and watch it develop into something interesting to read. What I didn't realize about myself is I didn't know I could create art.

I can crochet, I can sew, and I can cook. All of those skills are not necessarily considered art, but when they are combined, they can become a masterpiece. What talents are you hiding?

When I started writing stories for my first book and blog, I wasn't sure I could. The more I wrote, the more comfortable I became. It didn't matter if I had all the spelling and grammar correct, I just started writing. It turns out I can write more than poetry. My passion for writing has narrowed to writing to inspire others to grow in their faith in God and themselves. I especially like writing messages of hope.

What secret messages have you stored away? What skills do you have that can help you unpack your dreams?

Today's Journal Entry

Make a list of your gifts and talents. Put a star by the ones you want to develop and share with others.

Do you need to take classes to help you get started or begin again sharpening those skills?

Re-write your original encouragement statement or write a new one. If you're feeling creative, try turning it into a poem.

Day 11

CLEAN OUT YOUR CLOSET

YESTERDAY, we looked at what you have and can use. Now let's look at what needs to go. Every season most of us go through our closets to see what needs to be stored away or shifted to make room for the current season. Winter coats and boots get pushed to the back of the closet to make room for spring and summer attire. In the fall we store away swimsuits, sandals, and shorts to give way for warmer slacks and sweaters. Did you know that emotional baggage can hinder your dreams or crowd your thoughts so much that you can't think about your future?

So, what needs to go? I say we start with unforgiveness and regret. Holding on to past hurts and offences keep wounds open and erect walls that we may have a hard time maneuvering over. Making statements like, "I would have done _____ if _____ hadn't happened", are used by people who need an excuse not to succeed.

The authors of the resources I am suggesting today are experts on helping others "clean out their closets". Bernard Haynes (2014) gives a list of the things people do that sabotage their success. Among those are fear (of failure, moving, getting out of comfort zones), holding on to the past and unforgiveness. Joyce Meyers is one of my favorite speakers and authors and she has written books and devotionals about overcoming past hurts, forgiveness, bitterness, and rejection. All of these can hinder our growth and keep us from having the life we want and fulfilling our dreams.

TODAY'S JOURNAL ENTRY

Reflect on the Following:

What things are you holding onto that keep you from moving forward?

What steps can you take to clearing away the past so that you can have the future you want?

RESOURCES FOR CLEANING OUT YOUR CLOSET

10 Things You Must Stop Doing That Sabotage Your Success by Bernard Haynes

https://goodmenproject.com/featured-content/10-things-must-stop-sabotage-success-kcon/

The Poison of Unforgiveness by Joyce Meyers

http://www.joycemeyer.org/articles/ea.aspx?article=the_poison_of_unforgiveness.

Day 12
A New View

ONE of the most beautiful things I've ever seen is the sunrise after an overnight rain in the summer. I like how the sun glistens off the raindrops on the grass, trees, and crepe myrtle. The air even smells new.

It may be hard to envision such an image after a failed attempt at something meaningful, but it is possible. We are encouraged to view failure as an opportunity for growth. That may sound like a cliché, but it is true. We can learn so much about ourselves when we change our view about our mistakes. In *Five Ways to Make Peace with Failure*, Susan Tardanico, presents five vital truths about failure. My favorite is number five. She says:

> *5. Try a new point of view. Our upbringing – as people and professionals – has given us an unhealthy attitude toward failure. One of the best things you can do is to shift your perspective and belief system away from the negative* ("If I fail, it means I am stupid, weak, incapable, and am destined to fall short") *and embrace more positive associations* ("If I fail, I am one step closer to succeeding; I am smarter and more savvy because the knowledge I've gained through this experience").

Teaching myself to paint and draw has been so liberating for me. I make mistakes quite often. I don't scrap the project when I mess up, I try using my mistakes to make a complete work of art. Some of the sweetest compliments are about pictures that look just a little "off" to me.

Today's Journal Entry

How do you view failure in yourself? Others?

Write your favorite quotes about failure.

Resources for Gaining a New View After Failure

Five Ways to Make Peace with Failure

https://www.forbes.com/sites/susantardanico/2012/09/27/five-ways-to-make-peace-with-failure/#395a539d3640

How to Handle Failure Well

https://www.christiantoday.com/article/learning.how.to.handle.failure.well/64304.htm

Day 13
CAUTION: WALL AHEAD

NO ONE likes to anticipate failure or setbacks, but let's face it. The road to success is not smooth and without curves and detours. Planning ahead for what could go wrong is called being "proactive". According to Gollwitzer and Sheeran (2006), creating an "If-Then" plan can help us prepare for setbacks and failures. In their study they found that 70% of the people who made plans for what to do when facing obstacles were successful at completing their goals. The study implies "if-then planning substantially increases the likelihood of attaining one's goals" (p 98).

I remember teaching a strategy similar to this to the batterer's group I facilitated. The men learned how to recognize "red flag" words that triggered destructive behaviors towards their families. Once we recognized the red flag words, we started practicing what to do when the words were spoken. The more the men practiced appropriate responses the more they began to report different reactions when someone said things that would upset them.

Creating an "If-Then" plan for maintaining momentum when we face detours and failures can increase our potential for reaching our goals. Even if we don't find ourselves face to face with what could go wrong, it seems wise to have something in place when unexpected and unanticipated events throw us a curve ball.

Today's Journal Entry

Do you feel you are making progress in fulfilling your dreams?

How much time do you spend on your dreams each week?

What is keeping you from working on your dreams?

Write three "If-Then" statements. (Example: If I am distracted by the television, then I will turn it off until I have worked on my dream for 2 hours." "If I miss my scheduled time to work on my dream, I will make it up by getting up 30 minutes earlier.")

RESOURCES FOR PREPARING FOR SETBACKS

IMPLEMENTATION INTENTIONS AND GOAL ACHIEVEMENT: A META-ANALYSIS OF EFFECTS AND PROCESSES

https://www.researchgate.net/profile/Peter_Gollwitzer2/publication/37367696_Implementation_Intentions_and_Goal_Achievement_A_Meta_Analysis_of_Effects_and_Processes/links/59d91a24a6fdcc2aad0d8c1f/Implementation-Intentions-and-Goal-Achievement-A-Meta-Analysis-of-Effects-and-Processes.pdf

How to Use If Then Planning to Achieve Any Goal

http://99u.com/articles/7248/how-to-use-if-then-planning-to-achieve-any-goal

Day 14
ANOTHER DAY OF REST

I HAVE learned to enjoy days of rest. I often take myself on a personal retreat. The retreat may just be in my art studio where I create something inspiring or visiting the local hobby store. I may not buy anything, but I love walking up and down the aisles to see if I get an inspiration. There are other days I go get a pedicure and press the ON button of the massage chair remote. Still other days, I take road trips with my family to do something fun. My favorite retreats are the ones where we do something new or something we haven't done in a long time.

Plan to do something new this time. Take a nature drive to admire the change in the season or look at the shapes of trees along the path. I love to look at trees. They all are different, they all have a purpose, and they all seem to keep reaching for the sky. Even trees that look dead still stand tall as if to say, "Nothing is going to keep me from my destiny."

You might not be into nature, so do something you always wanted to do that doesn't cost much. Personal retreats should be stress-free and beneficial.

Today's Journal Entry

Reflect on the Following:

- How can you benefit from slowing down?
- What did you do to relax?
- How did you share yourself with others?
- Write a plan for next week's day of rest.

Day 15
SPEED BUMPS & WALLS

Now that we are starting week three, you may find yourself faced with that wall I warned you about last week. No problem. We have a plan, right? Today is a challenge. Taking a day off was good, but something unimaginable may have caught you off guard. You didn't plan to hit a wall so soon. That's not necessarily a bad thing. Have you ever thought about using the wall as inspiration or a tool to getting to your destination?

I know that may sound strange, but consider this. If the wall you face today is a lack of resources, this could be just the motivation you need to create a budget for your dream. If the wall is a drought of new ideas for a marketing strategy, take an online course to learn how to use social media to advertise. If your wall is an unexpected meeting, use the short breaks to jot down ideas about how to make up the time lost during the meeting.

I think you get the idea. Our response to delays and setbacks should not be shutting down or giving up on our dreams. We have to use our creative thinking to get going again.

If you have hit wall, this is the best time to go back to the beginning of this journey to reflect on why you started. Review your motivational messages you wrote to yourself. If you haven't lost motivation yet, wonderful! Give yourself a high five.

This is a good place to create another motivational page in your journal. Decorate it this time with motivational and celebratory word pictures. This could be a mini vision board about your desired destination featuring what you have already accomplished, what adjustments you want to make, and any new ideas you want to focus on in the future.

Today's Journal Entry

Reflect on the Following:

- Name your wall or speed bump (if you have any).
- How can you use this delay to get moving again?
- List your accomplishments and any adjustments you want to make.
- Create a mini vision board.

Resource for Dealing with Setbacks

5 Ways to Stay Motivated when You Experience Setbacks

Brian Bagnall

https://www.huffingtonpost.com/brian-bagnall/5-ways-to-stay-motivated-_1_b_10664424.html

Day 16
STARTING AGAIN

THE journey to dreams often have setbacks, but setbacks don't always mean failure. Writing this book was fun, but very challenging. I teach school full time, write a blog, and am working on starting a virtual business. Someone asked me how I juggle all of it. I laughed because I don't juggle very well. One day I work on an isolated project. On another day I may work on all three. As you may suspect, I have small burnouts. Burnout for me looks like I have abandoned my dream, but actually I walk away from everything to focus on something totally unrelated.

That may sound contradictory to the purpose of this book, but it really isn't. Is your dream completely about you? Or, does your dream involve others? When your dream is accomplished, will someone else's life be changed?

Hopefully your dream involves touching lives in the world around you. If so, how can you know if what you are seeking will make a difference? You can know by spending time learning about who you want to influence. There is a famous quote by President Theodore Roosevelt that challenges the purpose for our dreams, especially if our goal is to change the world around us. He said, "People don't care how much you know, until they know how much you care." People won't know how much you care until you spend time with them, getting to know them.

As a creative person, it is very easy for me to go into my studio and work. I could literally spend days isolated with just my laptop, canvases, journals, and other crafts. But if I don't spend time with others, I am cutting off my sources of inspiration and I am limiting my sphere of influence. My time off from my projects aren't totally unrelated, but more of an exploration. I go explore the world around me, watch a documentary, read an article, or glance at the news headlines. Taking small detours helps me get a fresh perspective and affirms that the change I desire to see is necessary. I am then ready to start again. You may wonder how long it takes me to start again. That depends. The time ranges from few hours to a few weeks. But I always return with new energy and momentum.

Today's Journal Entry

Reflect on the following:
- Who will benefit from your dreams?
- How do you know your vision will make a difference?
- What can you do to learn about the lives you want to touch?
- Set a time limit for detours.

Resource for What You Can do During Detours

4 Ways You can Start Helping Your Community and Changing Lives

http://www.ifcs.org/news/4-ways-you-can-start-helping-your-community-and-changing-lives/

Day 17
SHARPEN YOUR SKILLS

NONE of us is born with all the knowledge we need to lead successful lives. Some people have natural instinct and abilities to do things, but everyone is designed to learn.

Today is a day to evaluate, reflect, and connect.

Evaluate:
- List the skills you need to accomplish your dreams.
- List the resources you need.
- List the people who can help you reach your goals.

Reflect:
- How many of those skills do you already have?
- How have you used the resources already have?
- Who have you encountered on your journey with the same vision as you?

Connect:
- Enroll in classes if you need new skills.
- Create a budget for your dream including ways to finance future projects.
- Contact people you know with similar goals.

- Watch videos by those who inspire you or read their books.

When we evaluate, reflect, and connect we are practicing the change or success we want. We are sharpening our skills and learning new ones. We are constantly growing and modeling the change we want to see in the world.

Today's Journal Entry

Reflect on the following:

- What new things did you learn about yourself today?
- What new resources did you locate today?
- What new contacts did you make?
- How soon will you start your "class"? (Watching videos or reading books by those who inspire you.)

Resources for Sharpening Your Skills

This is intentionally blank. You know your skills better than I do. Make yourself a resource page at the back of your journal. I suggest using a variety of resources such as books, videos, websites, etc.

Day 18
SEND OUT INVITATIONS

HAVE you ever received a "Grand Opening" invitation in the mail from a new business in your community? They are reaching out to you for your support. They are inviting you to join them in making their business a success. Without community support, their doors would close very quickly.

Some businesses go as far as having preview days. They invite individuals to try their products or services in order to get their feedback. They roll out the red carpet to make their new customers feel welcome. There are huge discounts and freebies that encourage customers to return and tell their friends about them. The grand opening event is a very successful marketing strategy. It is an excellent way to gain support.

In order to accomplish what we long for we need to adopt some of those marketing strategies. We have to surround ourselves with people who will support and encourage us. We have to open ourselves up for feedback. Allowing others access to our dreams even at a limited level can be overwhelming and intimidating, but necessary.

In his classic book 7 Habits of Highly Effective People, Steven Covey describes this invitation as "synergy". Covey teaches that in order to be successful, we need to connect with others and invite them to come along side us to fulfill our dreams. I wish I could summarize this, but the following passage changed the way I look at inviting others into my dream life:

To put it simply, synergy means "two heads are better than one." Synergize is the habit of creative cooperation. It is teamwork, open-mindedness, and the adventure of finding new solutions to old problems. But it doesn't just happen on its own. It's a process, and through that process, people bring all their personal experience and expertise to the table. Together, they can produce far better results than they could individually. Synergy lets us discover jointly things we are much less likely to discover by ourselves. It is the idea that the whole is greater than the sum of the parts. One plus one equals three, or six, or sixty--you name it.

When people begin to interact together genuinely, and they're open to each other's influence, they begin to gain new insight. The capability of inventing new approaches is increased exponentially because of differences.

At first, I was hesitant to share my thoughts and ideas with others thinking they might steal my idea. But I soon discovered that I needed someone to hear my thoughts and give me feedback. I have learned to accept their critical feedback as well. Embracing synergy helps us build a team of support we cannot afford to ignore if we want to keep moving forward.

Today's Journal Entry

Reflect on the following:

- Who can you invite to join you on your dream journey?
- Whose dream or vision complement yours and you can merge your ideas into something wonderful?
- What is keeping you from opening yourself up to others?
- List your fears of sharing and make a plan to start with just one person to invite into your dream. Then invite others as you reach new levels of success.

Resources for Planning Your Grand Opening

7 Habits of Highly Effective People by Steven Covey

Day 19

PLAN A LAUNCH PARTY

EVERYBODY loves a good party. Celebrations stir up emotions of fulfillment and give us a sense of accomplishment. The goal for today is to plan how you will celebrate your successes and how you can celebrate the successes of others.

The following quote from Inc.com says it so well.

"Celebrating your wins not only feels great physically, but it reinforces the positive attitude and behavior you want to show up when you face a new challenge or opportunity."

I want to give you three reasons you should start planning your first celebration today.

1. You have been working very hard to unpack your dreams.
2. Your stamina needs encouragement.
3. You want to avoid burnout.

Working on accomplishing goals is hard work especially if you are working on doing things you once feared would never happen. The tasks you have faced can be emotionally draining and depleting of your energy. Depletion of your energy can lead to burnout. Once burnout sets in, you are in danger of retreating and losing ground for reaching our goal.

Today's Journal Entry

Reflect on the following:
- List your successes so far.
- List ways you can celebrate.
- Set a "celebration" date and invite someone to share it with you.
- Plan a party to celebrate reaching your ultimate goal.
- How can you reach out to someone who is working on their dreams? Invite them to a celebration hosted by you.

Resource that Encourage Frequent Celebration

Why You Should Celebrate Everything by Polly Campbell

https://www.psychologytoday.com/blog/imperfect-spirituality/201512/why-you-should-celebrate-everything

3 Reasons Celebrating Your Many Accomplishments Is Critical to Your Success by Bill Carmody

https://www.inc.com/bill-carmody/3-reasons-celebrating-your-many-accomplishments-is-critical-to-your-success.html

Day 20
NEW EQUIPMENT

YOU may have noticed that most of the resources suggested in this book require using the internet. That means you need access to technology. I'm a huge fan of using technology for practically every task. I remember when computers were first introduced at the police department where I worked. I was so excited and I was a natural. When individuals were able to buy personal computers, I was so excited. I got my first computer in 1994. It was expensive, but worth every penny. I was able to launch my first publishing project and I haven't stopped since.

I started with publishing papers and have since moved on to publishing videos and podcasts. I have learned on my journey that in order to keep up with the current generation of thinkers, I have to upgrade my skills and presentation. It isn't enough to know how to write, I also need to know how to publish, speak, and create opportunities to reach more people.

I recently met a woman in her mid-seventies who had the latest iPhone. She didn't know how to use it, but was willing to learn. She wanted access to teachings by her favorite speakers, but she didn't want to invest time in learning how to access YouTube on her phone. She would rather wait to catch the person on television or at a conference. She limited her ability to grow by refusing to upgrade with a tool she already owned.

Are you working with the right equipment? Having the right tools and using them is very important for moving forward.

Do you use what's available with enthusiasm or suspicion? If you have access to the internet then you probably have access to social media. I know many adults who are suspicious of social media. Social media can be a friend or foe. Using social media to reach others and share yourself in positive ways makes it your friend. Allowing social media to distract you from your purpose makes it your foe.

Today, your assignment is to explore what technology is available for you to reach your goal. Use Google or Safari to learn how technology can help you in your area of interest. You are certain to get references for social media. Click on what you find. You might be surprised by the number of people are interested in your ideas.

Do you need an upgrade? If you are not using technology yet, today is your day to give it a try. Your local library probably makes computers available to the public. Go use one to research your area of interest. See if you can locate books, magazines, or journals. Then see if you can access the internet to locate blogs. Using technology at the public library is free or very inexpensive and is a great way to introduce yourself to a new skill. Once you become comfortable, take a class at a community college. You won't be disappointed.

TODAY'S JOURNAL ENTRY

Reflect on the following:

- What new skills are you planning to pursue?
- How will you learn your new skills?
- Choose one social media platform to explore. Write down what you learn.
- If you need help, who can you ask to show you around your chosen social media platform?

RESOURCES FOR UPGRADING YOUR SKILLS

Why Social Media is Important by Lindsay Patton-Carson (2014)

http://udemyblog.wpengine.com/why-social-media-is-important/

Day 21
REST FROM YOUR WORK

WE have reached the end of week three. Give yourself a pat on the back and then take a rest from your work. Do something today that inspires you, gives you peace, or spend time with someone who makes you laugh.

There are so many reasons we should laugh that I am going to let the experts have this chapter. The following links are a collection of articles and podcasts that will brighten your day. Take time today to try a few of them out. At the end of the day write a reflection about how you spent today and make a plan for your next day of rest.

- Laughter is Good for the Soul (Podcast)
  http://familylifetoday.com/program/laughter-is-good-for-the-soul/
- 5 Fascinating Reasons Why Laughing is Awesome for Your Health by Sammy Nickalls
  https://inspiyr.com/laughing-good-for-you/
- Dr. Don Colbert (video)
  https://www.youtube.com/watch?v=eUFr3CO_Zjw
- Michael, Jr. Comedian (video)
  https://www.youtube.com/watch?v=-rqz7LjH7aU

Day 22
REFLECTION

WE'VE made it to the last week of the beginning of your journey forward. Now that we're here, this is a good time to go back to reflect on the progress you've made. Reflection is important because it gives us an opportunity to evaluate what works and what doesn't work. When we pause to reflect over our projects, we find things that may need adjusting or eliminating. Today we are going to look at what works.

Look back over the last three weeks and make a list of tasks or goals you have completed. Then create a list of strategies you used to complete them. What would you change? What would you add? Are there days you need to revisit?

As you spend time reflecting over this journey, re-evaluate your purpose and make notes about any shifts in your thinking. Have you changed your mind about what you want to accomplish? If so, you are not alone.

It takes courage to admit you no longer have passion for pursuing particular goals. Many people think they have to continue a path that isn't working for them to save face. They want to avoid appearing indecisive or unreliable. To the contrary, realizing that something is no longer needed or of interest shows integrity and character.

The purpose of the research assignments in Days 17 through 20 is to give you an opportunity to explore the benefits of your dream. You may have found that your dream or purpose is outdated and needs to adjust to meet modern society. Someone else may have already addressed the needs you want to address and their work is very effective. Your dream could be adjusted to support them in their endeavors. You may have a fresh idea to share with them and can partner with them to improve what they are doing.

If this time of reflection uncovers deficiencies in your progress or plan, don't get discouraged. The beauty of having a moving forward journal is that it is a work in progress. You are the author of the journal and you determine how to proceed. You have choices. You can continue on the path you're on, or you can go back and start again.

Today's Journal Entry

Reflect on the following

- List accomplishments and strategies, you used to succeed.
- List any adjustments you want to make and strategies to make those adjustments.
- After revisiting your journal entries for the previous three weeks, list any new things you have learned about yourself.
- List how you will use the new things for future goals.

Resources that Support Changing Your Mind

Why You Shouldn't Feel Guilty When You Change Your Mind about What You Want to Do by Kat Boogaard

https://www.themuse.com/advice/why-you-shouldnt-feel-guilty-when-you-change-your-mind-about-what-you-want-to-do

How to Set Goals for the Life You Actually Want by Stever Robbins

https://www.fastcompany.com/3029765/how-to-set-goals-for-the-life-you-actually-want

If you don't think you have a purpose start here:

What on Earth am I Here For? Purpose Driven Day 1 by Rick Warren

http://www.purposedriven.com/day1/

Day 23
THE POWER OF "NO"

ON Days 5 and 10 we made a list of things we needed keep or needed to eliminate from our lives. Is there something you got rid of that you needed? Or, is there something else you need to eliminate?

Before we reach the final day of this course, I want to remind you that it is okay to say "No". In fact, saying "no" may be the best gift you can give yourself and your loved ones. When I facilitated a support group for batterers, we spent an entire week on saying "no" because we often find ourselves frustrated because we are overwhelmed. Once we get overwhelmed with life expectations, fulfilling the needs of others, or trying to meet our own expectations, we tend to shut down. We can avoid sabotaging our own success by simply saying "no".

It's okay to say no to things that consume your time, especially if what's being presented is unnecessary. For example, you can say "no" to a dinner party invitation. You can say "no" to a shopping spree with friends just to relieve stress especially if your goal is to save money. You can say "no" to that root beer float when you know your goal is to lose five more pounds.

Give yourself permission to say "no" and you will discover you have more time to fulfill your purpose. You will rest better and others will appreciate the more relaxed version of you.

Today's Journal Entry

Reflect on the following:

- Make a new list of what you need to eliminate from your life.
- Identify what plans you have already made that you need to say "no" to and practice saying no before making the calls.
- Identify days on your schedule when you are able to say "yes". Mark those days on a personal calendar so that you have a reference point when you are asked to do something that may take time from your purpose.

Resources for Learning to Say No

5 Reasons Why You Need to Get Better at Saying No by Michael Hyatt
https://michaelhyatt.com/5-reasons-why-you-need-to-get-better-at-saying-no/

Boundaries Updated and Expanded Edition: When to Say Yes, How to Say No to Take Control of Your Life by Dr. Henry Cloud and Dr. John Townsend
https://www.amazon.com/Boundaries-Updated-Expanded-When-Control/dp/0310351804/ref=pd_sim_14_3?_encoding=UTF8&psc=1&refRID=10SKXRWK2VQZN0PCM1DB

Day 24
Gift of Delays

Often when we begin to work toward fulfilling our dreams or reaching a goal, we find ourselves on a path leading us away from our destination. We get delayed by life events or mistakes we make. We may even get sidelined due to rejection. That doesn't mean the dream is over and not for us. It is merely a signal we may need to take a time out.

I put extreme pressure on myself to write this book within the first three months of 2017. I am laughing now because it is now the end of November 2017. Since I am a school teacher who is off for three months in the summer, I postponed working on this project until summer when I realized that I wasn't going to meet my deadline. Well, I missed my second deadline. At first, I felt guilty about the delays, but I eventually realized that those delays were a gift.

Every time I start working on the book, I read the previous days I have written and discover errors I've made or gain new insights about areas of my life where I can use the principles in this book. I could easily have forced myself to sit at my laptop and plow through the writing process until I finished by my first deadline. I gave myself permission to wait because I wanted to finish strong. To me there is nothing worse than watching a movie where the previews are better than the entire movie.

My decision to slow down this time wasn't due to procrastination; it is called delayed gratification. I have learned to enjoy delays like this because the end result will be for my good verses hindering my progress.

Rushing through a project doesn't always end well, so there are times when we may need to extend our deadline.

Today's Journal Entry

Reflect on the following:

- Is your deadline too rigid? Check your deadline, evaluate your progress, and determine if you need an extension.
- Set your extension date.
- Record any changes or adjustments you want to make.

Resource to Consider When Facing Delays

5 Strategies for Delayed Gratification and Why You Should Do It by Brendan Baker

http://www.startofhappiness.com/power-delayed-gratification/

Day 25
SHARE THE WEALTH

NOW that you have started this journey, you have something to offer. You have reached a measure of success because you have decided to move forward. You have learned something about yourself and the process for having the life you want.

The best way to keep up momentum is to share what you have learned. You can share with your most intimate friends, family members or volunteer to speak at a local non-profit organization. You will be surprised how many people in residential facilities need someone to point them in the right direction for changing their circumstances.

Your dream may not be public speaking and it may scare you to even think about it. You don't have to go "public". You could offer to lead a group at your community library, community center, religious organization, or senior citizen facility.

You could even create something in print for people to read or publish a podcast about your process to fulfilling your dream. Whatever you decide to do, make giving back part of your dream. We have enough people in our world looking out for number one. The world needs what you have to offer and someone is just waiting for that special something you're holding onto.

Today's Journal Entry

Reflect on the following:

- Make a list of organizations or groups who would welcome your visit.
- Make contact with the organization or group leaders.
- Find someone who can help you start a blog or website. You can reach people worldwide when you're online.

Day 26
STEPPING OUT

A new wardrobe is not only what you wear on the outside, it is also what's on the inside. When you start recognizing your successes, you will start feeling more confident about what you've set out to do. As you start walking in confidence, your perspective will change, your thought processes will change, and your physical appearance will change slightly. Others will notice. Why?

Because you are now experiencing the freedom to be yourself, you true self. You are no longer walking in the valley of regret and unfulfilled expectations. Even if you think your dream is insignificant, you will experience a type of transformation that can only be explained by the hope that is now radiating from you.

It is important to remember success is a process. As you move toward your goal, there will be ups and downs, but you can still walk with confidence because your dreams are now within reach. You are no longer hidden beneath regret and disappointment. You've taken a step of faith to stretch out your hand toward a future of full of possibilities.

When others ask you about what is different, you need to be prepared for what you are going to tell them. Now is not the time for selfish bragging. You didn't make it this far on your own. Today is another day of reflection and thinking forward. Have you ever watched an awards show on television where individuals received an award recognizing their accomplishments? They always have a speech prepared. Do you think they spontaneously delivered those speeches? They did not. They knew ahead of time there was a possibility they would be selected and were ready when their name was called.

Today you are going to write your "acceptance speech". Even if your dreams aren't for public recognition, you are going to be recognized. The reward for starting to pursue the dreams of your heart is being able to personally recognize your progress and having others recognize the great strides you are making. Public figures often make lists of people to recognize. They may include their creator, their mentors, and family members who stood by them as they struggled to achieve their goals.

You may feel strange writing an acceptance speech for this stage in your journey, but it will give you motivation to be prepared for success. It strengthens your faith and helps shape your attitude into one of thankfulness and generosity. You may feel like you are bragging to talk about your accomplishments, but there are times when you have to put aside your modesty in favor of possibly inspiring someone to get moving forward. That's why we are going to practice answering questions you are sure to encounter as others notice you are moving forward.

Today's Journal Entry

Write a response to the following questions:
- What's different about you?
- You don't have the same attitude as before. What happened?
- How did you do that (reach the goal)?

Day 27
LEGACIES & LEGENDS

PEOPLE often plan for their future by making plans for taking care of their families after they pass away. Others make living wills and pass things on before the end of their time. After all the planning and bequeaths are met, individuals aren't remembered most by the physical things they leave. They are remembered by the lives they touched, the trails they blazed, and the life adventures that outlive them.

My grandparents have been gone for quite some time, but I have distinct memories of times I spent with them. I could tell some very funny and inspiring stories about them all. Even my paternal grandfather who had very limited contact with me left something for me to embrace as an adult. I am sure some of the stories I could tell would seem insignificant to all of them, but they shape who I have become. They all have left a legacy that is unique to their personalities and gifts.

I think I learned to be a storyteller from all of them. I have a quiet personality like my maternal grandfather. I am also creative like him. I can bake delicious desserts like my paternal grandmother. I can bake mouth-watering buttermilk biscuits like my maternal grandmother. I learned the value of integrity and loyalty to my family and friends from my paternal grandfather. I have other family members and friends who have left legacies that have made a permanent impact on my life.

How do you want to be remembered? What footprints do you want to leave? People sometimes think that writing wills and legacies are a sign that death is coming, but that is a false assumption. Planning for the future and being intentional about impacting the future is a blessing. It gives hope to others. It creates a permanent blueprint or testimony for others to follow.

Leaving a legacy of hope is so important. There are many people who feel hopeless and insignificant. Many are looking for proof that it is not too late for them to have the life they want—to fulfill their dreams. That is why people write books. They not only want to entertain. They want to leave something of themselves.

There is a book inside of you and someone will want to read it. You don't have to publish it, but you should write it. Writing your story describing your hopes, dreams, setbacks, and victories can be just the motivation others need.

Your "book" doesn't have to be a book. It can be a video or a digital document that inspires. Since you are the author and creator, you can make it funny or serious. You can make it as long or short as you want. You can determine what goes in it. The power is in your hands.

Today your assignment is to start writing your story. You can tell one short story or one long story about why you decided to unpack your dreams at this stage in your life. You can share a story about an inspiring moment in your life. Tell a story about how you overcame a setback, accepted and met a challenge, or made a decision at a major crossroad in your life.

TODAY'S JOURNAL ENTRY

Make a plan to write your story and how you will share it with your family & friends.

Day 28
PAUSE BUT DO SOMETHING

THIS is another day of rest. I hope you planned big for this one because we are two days away from the end of a beautiful beginning. As you spend this day relaxing and doing something you enjoy, remember to pray for someone other than yourself or those close to you. Take time to affirm someone and be a source of encouragement to someone who is feeling discouraged. Give someone a reason to smile.

At the end of today, reflect on the following:

- Who has been the greatest influence in your life?
- How can you honor them on this journey?
- How can you pay forward what you have learned from starting this journey?

Day 29
FORWARD TOGETHER

Now that you have spent the last four weeks unpacking your dreams, your life will never be the same again. You will never be content to just let life happen without getting involved. It is very important that you keep moving forward. It is equally important to team up with someone on your journey forward.

We were not created to do life alone. There is a proverb that says, "Keep company with the wise and you will become wise…" (Proverbs 13:20). We need others to help us keep moving forward. There is power in friendship.

I have friends who are constantly encouraging me to write, paint, and teach. When I get discouraged, they remind me that I am not alone and that what I do is important. They remind me that my dreams matter and they don't let me quit when I make a mistake. They help me process my mistakes and they quote me at times to remind me of my purpose.

Who are you walking with? Do you have friends who will help you reach your goals? Have you shared your dreams with your friends? Sometimes we don't have the support we need, because we keep our hopes and dreams secret. We may be afraid that others will laugh at us. People who care about us and are loyal to us will walk with us on our journey forward. They will remind us of the destination and when we leave the path they will serve as our navigators.

TODAY'S JOURNAL ENTRY

Reflect on the following:
- Make a list of your reliable friends.
- Who do you want to share your dreams with?
- Make plans to meet with them to invite them into your future.

Day 30
LAUNCH DAY

TODAY IS THE DAY! You've accomplished something wonderful. You completed the beginning of the journey toward your future. Notice I didn't say you have arrived. This is only the beginning. There is so much more life for you to live. There are so many lives you need to touch.

What's next? That's an easy question to answer. You keep going. Every day is an opportunity to do something amazing.

Keep moving forward.

Start the journey over as often as necessary, but don't stop moving.

TODAY'S JOURNAL ENTRY

Reflect on the following:
- What has been your greatest challenge so far?
- List the benefits for continuing on this process.
- Create a celebration page. Include pictures, favorite quotes from the resources, and quotes from people who recognize what you have accomplished.

The Truth about Living Your Dreams

Changing your life is a process.

It would be wonderful if we could wake up one day with a made-up mind that we are going to be successful and find ourselves in the exact place we want to be. But in reality, every successful person faces ups and downs. It is our response to those ups and downs that determines the outcome of our change.

I know at least three people who were more than 200 pounds overweight who wanted to lose weight without surgery. One person has gained an additional 120 pounds. One has lost 150 pounds and the other fluctuates. All of them report struggling to stick to their plan but the difference in all of them is the young lady who has lost 150 pounds, is tracking her progress, her emotions, and successes, and she has a support system.

I also know people who are substance abusers who want to change their lives. Several have completed substance abuse programs. A few enrolled, but didn't finish. All of them report having setbacks. The young man who has been successful in quitting, decided to keep a journal of his journey. He can recognize triggers, knows people to avoid, and has a list of people who will walk with him when he feels like giving up.

I have also met people who decided in their later years to go after their dreams. Some get started, but stop because someone told them they are too old. Others have continued and have successfully finished school, started businesses, and begun new careers. The difference in their circumstances is believing in their ability to accomplish their goals, having a support system, and creating a plan for recovering from disappointment.

I went back to college at age 30. I was a widow supporting three young children with social security benefits. Those were the most challenging years of my life. I was very fortunate to have family support, friends who encouraged me not to give up, and I kept journals that helped me stay focused on my goals. It was during this time that I realized I could have the life I wanted if I didn't give up on myself, if I relied on the support from family and friends, and if I accessed other resources available to me.

I learned to say "no" to things that would hinder my progress. I discovered who to trust with my dreams, and who really isn't interested in my success. I learned to be grateful for my setbacks because there are lessons to learn in them. The most important lesson I learned is to trust God and to give thanks in all things. I also learned that my success triggers success for others.

My family and friends started making changes. People began to ask me for advice and to help them start working on their dreams. The first thing I tell anyone who asks me about how to get started is they must realize that nothing worth having comes easily. Change is a process that begins with a made-up mind.

If you are determined to have your dreams, then take them out. Take a good look at them and begin planning how you are going to reach them. You are not only going to need a plan for reaching your goals, but you will also need a plan for what to do when things get tough.

You can hire a life coach. But even with a life coach, you are going to have setbacks. You will need a plan for that. That is when you will need to become your own life coach. You're going to have to rely on your faith in your Creator and yourself to overcome your setbacks so that you can keep moving forward.

Appendix

A 5-S Framework for Success

The following framework helps me stay focused when I start a new project. I suggest creating a notecard for each "S" to hang in a prominent place or you may want to create a 5-S section in your journal.

Sight: See yourself being successful. Set goals for your future. You need a vision

- What does success look like to you?
- Where do you see yourself in two, three, five years?
- What legacy do you see leaving for your descendants?
- What mark would you like to make on the world?
- What will your footprints lead others to?

Shift: Change how you view failure and setbacks. Setbacks and failure can be overcome. View failures as opportunities for growth and don't let fear cloud your judgment or cast a shadow over your dreams.

- Write a message of encouragement to yourself and keep it readily available.
- Write three positive responses to negative feedback and disappointments.
- Write messages of hope to share with others when they experience failure or setbacks.
- Write a list of possible setbacks before starting a project and make a response plan for each.

- Write a description of your setbacks. Research and implement possible solutions or start fresh. Sometimes starting over is the best solution.

Start: Every journey has to start somewhere. You cannot be successful if you never take that first step.

- Start telling yourself you can succeed.
- Start everyday meditating on being a better you than you were the day before.
- Start every day with a clean slate for you and those around you.
- Start journaling the journey and keep good notes about what works and what doesn't work.
- Start building a support system and an accountability system with people who will encourage you and speak truthfully to you when you're tempted to give up.

Share: Share yourself with others. You may not think you have anything to give, but you do. Everyone was born with a purpose. If you had no purpose, you would not have been born.

- What were you created to share?
- How can your dream benefit others?
- Where can your gifts and talents best serve others?
- How will you pass along your legacy to your decedents?
- Who will you mentor to learn how to keep your dream alive?

Stand: Don't compromise your dreams or your purpose. When trouble comes, don't give up.

- Keep in contact with your support and accountability system when things are good or bad.
- Keep up-to-date on things that are happening around you.
- Keep looking for ways to improve.
- Keep a list of those who help you and remember to thank them quickly.
- Keep moving forward.

Believe in yourself and your Creator. Have integrity when going for your dream. There is no greatness when you step on people to get where you want to be. In the end you want your legacy to be one that helps, not hinders.

ABOUT THE AUTHOR

Cindy Mosley, M.Ed., is a professional educator. Mosley has facilitated dating and family violence support groups for teens, women and men. Mosley has conducted professional developments for effective learning practices and dating and family violence and sexual harassment prevention at various schools in East Texas. Cindy is the author of several books for teens and adults.

Contact Information:

    Email: cimoswritelife@gmail.com

Follow at:

    Blog: www.cimowrites.com

    Facebook: https://www.facebook.com/createwritelove/

    Twitter: https://twitter.com/ci_mosley

www.ingramcontent.com/pod-product-compliance
Lightning Source LLC
Chambersburg PA
CBHW052309300426
44110CB00035B/2261